The Little Christ-like Soldier

Anastasia Felix-Moore

WestBow Press books may be ordered through booksellers or by contacting:

WestBow Press
A Division of Thomas Nelson & Zondervan
1663 Liberty Drive
Bloomington, IN 47403
www.westbowpress.com
1 (866) 928-1240

Scripture taken from the King James Version of the Bible.

Scripture quotations taken from the Holy Bible, New Living Translation, Copyright © 1996, 2004. Used by permission of Tyndale House Publishers, Inc., Wheaton, Illinois 60189. All rights reserved.

ISBN: 978-1-4908-5726-8 (sc)
ISBN: 978-1-4908-5725-1 (e)

Library of Congress Control Number: 2014919101

Printed in the United States of America.

WestBow Press rev. date: 11/10/2014

WestBow
PRESS
A DIVISION OF THOMAS NELSON
& ZONDERVAN

Acknowledgements / Dedications:

Donny Moore my partner in life and for life.
My sons Adiel and Ezrael continue to be my inspiration.
My mother, Selma Frederick, who always believed and
reminded me that one day I would write a book.
Asha Thompson-Joseph for your support and inspiration.

Table of Contents

Stories

Poems

Selfish or Selfless?

(Philippians 2:5-11)

Once upon a time there was a King living in his kingdom. He was a good King and was well-respected, honoured and loved. Everything within his kingdom was splendid. There were beautiful mansions, delicious food, music and dancing, and abundant living. There was not a citizen in that kingdom who lacked anything, no one was sick or in pain, and no one in that kingdom ever died. That kingdom was called Heaven.

One day the King looked over to another domain called Earth. On Earth some people were sick and suffering. Some persons had no homes to live in and lived on the streets. There were persons who did not have any food to eat for many days because they were so very poor. The worse part however, was that many of Earth's inhabitants were dying, both young and old people, and were going to an awful place called hell.

The King loved all people and wanted them to live with Him in His Kingdom. So the King sent His only son Jesus to Earth to die, so that Earth's inhabitants could live in His kingdom. Jesus the Son left all the riches of the Kingdom of Heaven and came to Earth. Jesus who did nothing wrong, took the punishment for those who did do wrong. The King so loved Earth's people, that He sent His only Son Jesus, to die in our place, so that we can live with Him in His kingdom forever.

Memory Verse: John 15:13
Greater love hath no man than this, that a man lay down his life for his friends. (KJV)
Prayer: Heavenly Father, I thank you for making me your child and receiving me into your kingdom. Amen.

That's Impossible!

(Joshua 10)

"That's impossible" shouted 4 year old Devon.

"Absolutely impossible!" agreed his 6 year old brother Dave.

"Are you sure mom, did that really happen?" asked their 8 year old sister Jenny.

"With God all things are possible, children", replied their mother Selma.

Selma, the children's mother was reading to them a bed time story. The story was about a brave young man named Joshua. Joshua at that time was the leader of the Israelite people. He was following God's command to take possession of the land which God had promised to the nation of Israel. God gave the promise to them through their fore-father Abraham. On this land they were to build their homes, farms, market places and places of worship. Joshua a descendent of Abraham, and the successor after Moses, was leading the fight against the enemies of Israel. 5 Amorite kings from 5 different nations came together and combined their armies to war against the Israelites. In total, these 5 armies could number in the hundreds of thousands.

"5 armies against one!" exclaimed Devon.

"The Israelites are sure to be defeated," remarked Jenny, sadly.

"What happened mom?" asked Dave.

"Let's read on," responded their mother.

The Lord told Joshua not to be afraid, because God was going to help them fight. Joshua launched a surprise attack on the Amorites armies, and they panicked. While the warriors fought with their swords, the Lord helped Israel, killing many of the Amorites by pitching huge stones from Heaven, like a terrible hail storm. That day Joshua prayed to the Lord before all the Israelite people. He asked God to let the mid-day sun keep shining, even though it should be evening time for the sun to set, and later night time, for the moon to come out. God listened to Joshua and the sun kept shinning on, and the day light lasted well into the night time. There has never been a day like that before or after it.

For with God, nothing shall be impossible!

Memory verse: Joshua 1:9
This is my command-be strong and courageous! Do not be afraid or
discouraged. For the Lord your God is with you wherever you go. (NTL)
Prayer: Lord I pray for the peace of Jerusalem.

Calming the Storm

(Luke 8:22-25)

It was a picturesque evening with the sun setting beautifully in the sky. What a better way to spend the evening than to go for a boat ride across the lake. Jesus said to His disciples, "Let us go over unto the other side of the lake". They all agreed and got into a ship. The cool breeze and rocking of the boat on the water would cause anyone to fall asleep. So Jesus fell asleep. Suddenly the sky began to blacken, thunder roared bursting forth from the sky, and lightning struck. The wind began tossing and howling and the waves hit against the ship growing bigger and higher. The ship began taking in water.

"A storm! A STORM! WE'RE GOING TO DIE!" panicked someone.

"Oh God, help us. I...don't... want... to... die", cried another disciple hysterically.

"JESUS! JESUS! Come and save us!" pleaded another disciple, as they shook Him.

Jesus arose and spoke to the raging wind and the water in the lake saying, "Be still."

Immediately the storm ended and there was calm and peace.

Memory verse: Phil 4:7
And the peace of God, which passeth all understanding, shall keep your hearts and minds through Christ Jesus.(KJV)
Prayer: Lord Jesus, help me not to be afraid, knowing that you are with me always.

Earthquake!

(Acts 16:25-36)

The Apostle Paul and Silas were going to prayer meeting one day. A girl who had an evil spirit in her like a witch started mocking them. Paul became so tired of her mocking that he commanded the evil spirit in her to come out of her, in the name of Jesus. Instantly the evil spirit left her. However, the people she was working for became angry as she was no longer making money for them by fortune telling. So enraged were her bosses that they told lies about Paul and Silas to the authorities, who threw then into prison. The jailor put them into the inner dungeon and chained their feet.

In prison, hours passed and Paul and Silas were singing and praying to God. At 12:00 mid-night everything began to shake. Just imagine everything around you shaking, chairs, bed, walls, cars, buildings, even the very ground that you stand upon. Earthquake! Everything was shaking so vigorously that the prison doors flew open and the chains on each prisoner were broken.

The jailor was awakened by the shaking. When he saw all the prison doors wide open, he just wanted to die. He knew he would be blamed for the prisoners going free. He drew his sword to kill himself, but Paul and Silas quickly shouted, "We are all here, do yourself no harm". The jailor put on the lights and trembling, he fell on his knees and asked Paul and Silas, 'What must I do to be saved?' They answered him, " Believe in the Lord Jesus Christ and you shall be saved, you and your household."

After the Jailor and his family received Jesus into their hearts, they were baptised. Paul and Silas were then released from prison.

Memory verse: Acts 16: 31
And they said, Believe on the Lord Jesus, and you will be saved, along with everyone in your household. (NLT)
Prayer: Lord Jesus I believe in you and I receive you into my heart. Thank you for saving me.

The Fiery Furnace

(Daniel 3)

Have you ever seen a house or car ablaze? Can you imagine being in the midst of a blazing hot fire, that burns up anything close to it. Three young friends found themselves in this situation. Their names were Shadrach, Meshach and Abednego. You might think that they must have committed a terrible crime for the King to command that they be thrown into the fiery furnace. That was not the case. These young men did not kill or hurt anyone, neither did they steal anything. In fact they did nothing wrong.

The King Nebuchadnezzar had a gigantic gold statue erected where all could see. He commanded that at the sound of certain musical instruments, everyone should bow and worship the golden image. However, these three friends refused to bow and worship the golden image. When it was reported to the king that these three Hebrew boys did not bow, the King became so furious, he sent for them. The friends told the King that they would only worship and obey God. The king, infuriated by their stance, threatened to throw them into the fiery furnace.

The boys replied, "The God whom we serve is able to save us from the fiery furnace, but even if He does not choose to deliver us, we still will not worship any other gods."

King Nebuchadnezzar became so angry you could see the rage on his face. He commanded that the furnace be heated up seven times hotter than usual. He called for the strongest men in his army to tie up the three Hebrew boys and throw them into the fiery furnace. The furnace was so terribly hot that the soldiers, who threw the boys in, got burned and died.

Suddenly, the king was astonished, he said, "Didn't we throw three young men into the furnace, with their hands and feet tied? Why am I seeing four men walking around in there? And the fourth man looks like God! Shadrach, Meshach and Abednego come out here!" the king shouted.

The three Hebrew boys walked out of the fiery furnace. No part of their bodies got burnt, not even their clothing, and they did not even smell like smoke.

King Nebuchadneezar declared to everyone, "Praise the God of Shadrach, Meshach, and Abednego."

Memory Verse: Ps. 91:3
For He will rescue you from every trap and protect you from deadly disease (NLT)
Prayer: Lord deliver us from all evil, Amen.

A talking donkey!

(Numbers 22-24)

God had promised Israel, His chosen people through Abraham, that He would give them a land called Canaan. This would be their home land, where they would establish their communities to live in. The land was inhabited by various people who became afraid of the Israelites because God was with them.

One such nation was Moab, and their King at that time was called Balak. Balak sent for the prophet Balaam, to pronounce curses upon the Israelites so that they would not defeat the Moabites in war. King Balak however, did not know that Balaam the prophet could only bless whom God told him to bless, and curse those God told him to curse. God told Balaam that He had blessed the Israelites so no one could curse them.

King Balak promised Balaam great wealth and honour, if he cursed God's chosen people. Balaam got up the next morning and decided to go with the King's messengers. God became extremely angry because Balaam disobeyed Him, and sent an angel to destroy Balaam. While Balaam was riding upon his donkey, his donkey saw the angel with his sword drawn to kill Balaam, and so the donkey moved aside and went into a field. Balaam did not see the angel, and so he hit the donkey for moving aside from the path. Again the donkey saw the angel with his sword drawn, and so he passed so very close to the wall that Balaam's foot got crushed. Balaam again, did not see the angel and he struck the donkey a second time. When the donkey saw the angel about to kill Balaam with his sword, the donkey collapsed under Balaam. Balaam struck the donkey a third time, for he still could not see the angel.

God then opened the donkey's mouth and caused him to talk to Balaam. The donkey said, "Master Balaam I have been your faithful donkey for many years now, why did you strike me these three times?"

Balaam replied furiously, "You are being disobedient to me, you foolish animal. Why are you going where I did not send you?"

"Master Balaam, I saw the angel with his sword drawn about to kill you, so I moved away" replied the donkey, apologetically.

Finally God opened Balaam's eyes and for the first time he saw the angel.

Memory verse: Numbers 23:19
God is not a man, that he should lie; neither the son of man, that He should repent: hath he said, and shall He not do it? Or hath He spoken, and shall he not make it good? (KJV)
Prayer: Lord help me to walk in obedience to you at all times.

Jesus is my Cousin!

(Luke 1:57-80)

Wouldn't you be all excited and boastful if you had a famous and powerful relative or friend? If your close relative like your father or mother was the Prime Minister or President of a country wouldn't you go about and tell everyone?

John, (John the Baptist) was the cousin of Jesus. He never one day boasted of his kinship to Jesus. Rather, his ministry was to point everyone to Jesus the Messiah. Jesus is the promised One, the Anointed One. John was called the fore-runner of Jesus and his message to everyone was, "Prepare ye the way of the Lord, make His path straight". He told people to turn away from sinful deeds and to look to Jesus for their salvation. He was the voice of one crying in the wilderness, "Repent and be baptised, for the kingdom of Heaven is at hand". John was called the prophet of the Most High God, and he was spiritually strong. Yet he lived in the wilderness and was quite humble. He informed everyone that he was not the Christ. He humbly stated that he was not worthy to even untie Jesus' sandals' straps.

Jesus declared that John was the greatest prophet who ever lived. However, a wicked queen named Herodias was upset with John's preaching because she did not want to turn from her sinful behaviour. That evil queen had John's head cut off for preaching the good news about Jesus Christ.

Memory verse: Phil 2:3
Let nothing be done through strife or vainglory; but in lowliness of mind let each esteem other better than themselves. (KJV)
Prayer: Lord bless and protect the men and women everywhere who are preaching the good news about Jesus Christ.

Food for growth

(Philippians 4:6-8)

As a child I often enjoyed looking at the cartoon "Popeye". Popeye was skinny and did not seem to have much physical strength. However his adversary Bluto was strong, muscular and boastful. Popeye liked the girl Olive and would try to impress her, but Bluto would always show up and try to steal Popeye's girl. This would lead to a physical fight, and Bluto would appear to emerge the winner. Just when everybody thought Bluto had won the fight and the girl, Popeye would start to think about spinach. The more he thought about spinach, the more his confidence grew that he could defeat Bluto. Popeye would think so hard about Spinach that he would either muster up the strength to go get a can of spinach, or the can would roll towards him. As Popeye began to feed on the spinach, his muscles would grow bigger and bigger, and his strength would increase. He would eventually become so strong that he would indeed take Bluto down and get his girl.

This cartoon reminds me of how we ought to feed on God's word to become strong in Christ. The way we feed on God's Word is by reading and practicing it. We must not worry about the situation we are facing, but think about God's promise of deliverance and victory. As we meditate upon God's Word, we will become stronger and grow spiritual muscles to defeat our enemy, the Devil.

Memory Verse: Neh. 8:10
...For the joy of the Lord is your strength. (KJV)
Prayer: Lord Jesus, help me always to remember that my only enemy is the devil.

A Happy Ending!

(James 1:2-18)

Have you ever looked at a movie, any movie? What's your favourite? I'm sure if given the opportunity you would tell us all about it. What makes one movie different from the other is the plot or story line, what the movie is all about. I have seen many different types of movies. Comedies are those movies that really make you laugh. Horror movies have plots about terrible events like murders and can make you very afraid. Romance movies have story lines about how people in relationships treat each other and demonstrate their love for each other.

Every great movie has a challenge that the main character must overcome in order for there to be a happy ending. In the book of James, God tells us that in life we will all have challenges to overcome, in order to see our happy ending. At times, life may be like a comedy when everything is all good and we are happy all of the time. At another time though, we may be facing a horrible situation like the murder of a close relative or friend. In another season we may fall in love and get married and start a family. There may sometimes be periods of terrible disease and sickness. This is what the book of James calls 'divers temptations'. Whatever the challenge life brings us, we must understand that God is taking us through it to test our faithfulness to Him. James assures us that if we stay focused on Jesus and let Him be our Healer in times of sickness, our Protector against the enemy, our Provider in times of need, and our Joy in times of sorrow. We must fix our minds on Jesus who is able to take us through each challenge and help us to pass each test.

Memory verse: James 1:12
Blessed is the man that endures temptation: for when he is tried, he shall receive the crown of life, which the Lord hath promised to them that love Him. (KJV).
Prayer: Father, help us to resist the devil when he tempts us.

Kidnapped!

(Psalms 23)

Susan awoke one Monday morning at the crack of dawn, as she usually did every morning. She began her daily routine by kneeling at her bedside and talking and listening to God. She thanked God for sparing her life to see another day, and for all the blessings He bestowed upon her and her family. She thanked Him for her family and friends, neighbours and even her enemies, and asked God to keep her safe throughout the day. Next, she read her favourite Psalms. Susan readied herself for school, left home and waited at the road side for a taxi.

Suddenly a white panel van pulled up in front of Susan, and without a single word, some men snatched her and pulled her into the van. The men gagged her mouth so she couldn't scream, blindfolded her and sped off. Susan was petrified. She couldn't believe that this was happening. She was being kidnapped. Instantly she started reciting the 23rd Psalm, over and over again. The kidnappers took Susan to an unknown house where they bound her hands and feet and kept her in a locked room. Thank God she was given sufficient food and water to survive.

After several days Susan was released into the streets of a well- known village, unharmed. She made her way to the police station, told the police her story and they reunited her with her family.

Susan's family, friends and church members were praying for her safe return, without stopping. They were extremely happy and thankful to God that she was alive and unharmed. When Susan was asked what kept her strong in such a terrifying situation she answered,

"Psalms 23."

Memory verses: Psalms 27:1 The Lord is my light and my salvation; whom shall I fear? The Lord is the strength of my life; of whom shall I be afraid? (KJV).
Prayer: Dear Lord, protect and keep me safe each day.

I'm too Busy!

(Luke 10:38-42)

Christmas time in Trinidad and Tobago is the most wonderful time of the year. At this time there is just a joy and merriment in the atmosphere. Many people are extremely happy and enjoy giving gifts and sharing with those who are less fortunate. As a child growing up, Christmas time came with a lot of hustling, bustling and cleaning of course! This was the time to wash the windows, scrub the floors, paint the veranda, bake the fruit cake, pick the sorrel, shell the pigeon peas, and sweep the yard. Annually, people would become so engrossed in their preparations for Christmas day, that they paid little attention to the reason for the season. Christmas is really about celebrating the birth of Jesus into this world. God the Son became flesh and dwelt among us.

The whole hustle and bustle of Christmas reminds me of an account in the bible of two sisters named Martha and Mary. Jesus came to visit their home one day. Mary sat at Jesus' feet listening to all His teachings, while Martha was busy cooking and cleaning. Martha went to Jesus and complained, "Mary is only sitting down and I have to do all of the work. I have to prepare the meal, tidy the house, and wash the dishes. Mary is just sitting there doing nothing, absolutely nothing! Do you think that's fair, it's not fair at all! My Lord, tell her to get up at once and come and help me."

Jesus replied to Martha, "Martha, you are complaining a lot, and no-one asked you to do all of this. In fact, what Mary is doing is much better than what you're doing. All I really need you to do right now is to sit and learn from me".

Memory verse: Phil. 2: 14
Do all things without murmurings and grumbling (KJV)
Prayer: Lord help me to never become so busy that I forget all about you.

Forgiveness Unlimited

(Matthew 18:21)

Once upon a time there lived a king who decided to take an account of all his debtors, that is, all the persons who owed him money. The king soon realised that one particular servant owed him over one million dollars. Stop for a moment and think of what you would do if you realised that someone borrowed money from you and never paid it back. The king summoned his servant and threatened to sell him and all that he owned. Upon hearing this dreadful news, the servant fell at the king's feet and begged for mercy. The kind-hearted king had compassion on the servant and forgave him his debt.

When the servant left the king he went to his friend who owed him a few thousand dollars. He grabbed his friend by the throat and immediately demanded his money. His friend begged and begged for some more time to pay what he owed. The wicked servant had his friend arrested and thrown into prison, because he could not pay the debt.

When the king heard the news of what had happened, he was enraged. The servant whom he just forgave was unforgiving. He summoned the wicked servant and said, "I really cannot believe that you did not forgive someone who owed you a little bit of money. I had compassion and forgave you millions!"

The angry king sent the man to prison to be tortured until he was able to pay of his entire debt.

Memory Verse: Math 6: 12
And forgive us our debts as we forgive our debtors. (KJV)
Prayer: Lord forgive me for all that I have done that was not pleasing
to you, and help me to forgive those who do me wrong.

Don't you fall!

(2 Peter1:3-10)

"Ahhhh! Oouch!" These were the loud sounds that could be heard all the way down the streets whenever little Johny fell down. Johny was a young boy aged 4, and he had very skinny brown wobbly legs. Johny's old brother Andy was 6 . Often they would play together, running and riding their bikes. Johny was quite adventurous and loved to try out new tricks on his bicycle. His father recently taught him to ride his bicycle without the use of training wheels. Sure enough, when Johny tried to imitate his bigger brother while riding or running, he was certain to fall. To his parents, it seemed that there was no way to keep little Johny from falling.

No one likes to fall. A fall may result in small cuts and bruises, but a major fall can lead to serious injury or even death. There is another fall that can occur in our lives that results in spiritual disaster and destruction. This happens when we sin against God. God admonishes us that if we are careful to take certain precautions we shall never fall into sin and the traps of the enemy. God has given us everything we need to live a godly life. We receive the power to overcome evil the day we accept Jesus Christ as our Lord and Saviour. To save you from falling God says have faith in Him. Additionally, we must strive for moral excellence and integrity. Get to know God and His Word and exercise self-control. Patiently endure difficulties, while demonstrating godliness. Be kind, compassionate and show love to all. Strive hard to do these things and ...and you will never fall.

Memory verse: Jude 24
Now all glory to God, who is able to keep you from falling away and will bring you with great joy into his glorious presence without a single fault. (NLT)
Prayer: Lord I give you my life. Please keep me from falling.

What happens when we die?

(Luke 16:19-31)

Once upon a time there lived a rich man and another man called Lazarus. The rich man had the best clothes, ate the best of food and lived each day in luxury. At the gate to his home lay a beggar called Lazarus. Lazarus would beg for the scraps of food left over from the rich man. Lazarus' skin was covered in sores which dogs would often lick. Lazarus believed in Jesus but the rich man did not.

Eventually both men died. Lazarus was carried by angels to be with Father Abraham in the Kingdom of Heaven. The soul of the rich man who did not believe in Jesus, went to hell. In hell he was continually tormented in flames of fire. "Father Abraham, have mercy. Please, send Lazarus over here to dip the tip of his finger in water to cool off my tongue, pleeeease!" This was the plea of a rich man who died without accepting Jesus into his heart.

Abraham answered the rich man, "There is a great space between you and us. Those who are across here in Heaven cannot come over there and those across there tormenting in hell cannot come over here."

Memory verse: Hebrew 9:27
And as it is appointed unto men once to die, but after this the judgment. (KJV)
Prayer: Lord help me to live for Jesus and inherit eternal life.

Can you imagine?

(Revelation 21)

Close your eyes for one brief moment and imagine. What did you imagine? I imagined that I was in a place where there are mansions, and I own one! The street that ran along the front of my mansion was paved in gold! Gold I say! My mansion was built within a gated community, and there were many other mansions all around. The gate that led into this community was pearly and white. The walls of the city were made of jasper, a precious stone. And it seemed as though I was some kind of prince or princess, for I had a most beautiful crown. There was no need for the sun or the moon for the glory of God illuminated the city. The people were joyful and glad. No one was sick or in pain, and nobody ever died in that place!

As I opened my eyes I realised that the place that I had imagined is a place called Heaven. It is the most wonderful place, and it is all real and true. Jesus dwells in Heaven. He shall return one day to take those who believe on Him to live with Him in Heaven. Each person should accept Jesus into their hearts and live for Him here in the Earth. That's the only way we can return with Him to live eternally in Heaven, when He comes again.

Memory verses: John 14:1-2
Let not your heart be troubled, ye believe in God, believe also in me. In my Father's house there are many mansions: if it were not so, I would have told you. I go to prepare a place for you. (KJV)
Prayer: Lord Jesus help me to be ready for your second coming.

Crossing the Red Sea

(Exodus 14:13-31)

Walking across the Red Sea,
Must have been amazing.
Imagine a sea splitting open
For the Israelites to walk in.

How did they get there, one may ask?
Escaping Pharoah and his punitive task?
Years of bondage and slavery,
As promised, Yaweh did set them free.

They left as a nation strong and mighty.
With great possessions, they became very wealthy.
Thus said the Lord, let my people go!
Were the words Moses spoke to the harden Pharoah.

Taking all their possessions, Israel left in haste,
And with chariots of fire, Pharoah's army gave chase.
With their enemy behind and the Red Sea before,
Israel looked to God to open any door.

God split the Red Sea and they walked across,
With all their possessions, not a life was lost.
Imagine seeing huge whales and sharks,
A frightening sight for the weakened heart.

And dolphins jumping, octopuses galore,
When they all crossed over God shut the door!
Then Pharoah rushed in, his chariots with him,
Too bad for them all, for they couldn't swim.

Memory Verse: Exodus 14: 14
The Lord shall fight for you and ye shall hold your peace. (KJV)

Party!

(Luke 15:11-32)

Trinidadians use any excuse to have a party.
A child is born...party!
Someone dies, after funeral party!
Exams at school; cool down...party!
Pyjama and nightie... party!
Eat, drink and be merry,
And party, hearty, baby!

So too did the prodigal son,
He asked for his half of his father's kingdom,
His father did not even pass on,
And you know, he was the younger son.

So he packed up all his belongings,
And went where he did not belong.
And squandered all his inheritance,
On wine, woman and song!

Soon all of his friends were missing,
And all of his money too!
He did not have a place to live,
Now what was he to do?

So he spent his days begging,
But no one gave him alms.
Then he found himself feeding,
The pigs on someone's farm.

Finally he came to his senses,
And said to himself but wait.
I do not have to stay here,
Hopefully it's not too late.

So he got himself together,
And started on the track.
Homeward to his father,
To plead to take him back.

Yet while he was a long way off,
His father came to him running.
With tears in his eyes and joy in his heart,
His son he couldn't stop hugging.

Let the party begin, cook everything!
His father said rejoicing.
My son who was lost, has come back home,
Thank you Jesus for saving him.

Memory verse: Luke 15:18
I will arise and go to my father and will say unto him, Father
I have sinned against heaven, and before thee (KJV)

One man and one man alone.

(Romans 5:12-21)

By the actions of one man alone,
Sin and death entered the world.
The ancient anecdote is told,
In Eden's garden did it all unfold

That wicked devil did tempt Eve,
In her weakness she was deceived.
All his lies she did believe,
To God's word she did not cleave.

The forbidden fruit tasted sweet,
And Adam and Eve did both eat.
Their disobedience marked the fall,
And sin was imputed to all.

And now sickness and death has come,
Pain and sorrow, God curse the ground!
And labour has become hard,
All this made God very sad.

As promised, God sent His Son,
To offer reconciliation
And through the obedience of One,
Restoration and redemption has come.

Jesus Christ paid the ransom for all,
To redeem and restore man, after the fall.
Upon His name you must now call
His salvation is free to all.

Memory verse: Rom 5:20
But where sin abounded, grace did much more abound. (KJV)

You amaze me!

(Jeremiah 31:3)

I never met someone who...
Makes me feel the way you do,
You've completely captured my heart,
And I can't bear to be apart...
From you Lord.

At first I felt so unworthy...
As I thought if you knew the real me,
You'd turn away, never looking at me,
Because I felt so ugly.
I need you Lord.

Lord, you know me entirely,
Yet you beckon to me so sweetly,
You over shadow me with your mercy,
With loving kindness, you reached out and touched me.
Thank you Lord.

How could you love me so completely?
And speak of me affectionately,
Bestowing gifts upon me daily,
Lord your grace amazes me.
I love you Lord.

Memory Verse: Jer. 31:3
The Lord hath appeared of old unto me, saying, Yea,
I have loved thee with an everlasting love: therefore
with loving kindness have I drawn thee. (KJV)

You know me

(Psalms 139)

Lord you know me entirely,
My Spirit, my mind and body,
You've formed and fashioned me,
A design you created originally.

From my mother's womb at conception,
Intense consideration and reflection,
Took place in heaven by the Trinity,
To determine every detail about me.

Such knowledge is too wonderful,
And for this I am forever grateful.
You know all I think of and do,
No secret is kept from you.

Lord your Spirit dwells within,
Upon my head, your hand of blessing.
When certain things I don't understand,
I know that I was made by The I Am That I Am.

I am fearfully and wonderfully made,
God was careful to ensure no error was made.
How precious are His thoughts about me,
They cannot be numbered, as the sand in the sea.

Every day of my life you've written,
Each path that I take you've chosen.
And even before the world began,
My life was in your hand.

Memory verse: Ps. 139: 14
I will praise thee for I am fearfully and wonderfully made: marvellous
are thy works; and that my soul knoweth right well. (KJV)

Great Grace!

(2 Corinthians 7-10)

It's because of your grace Lord I am who I am.
Your grace has given me the ability to stand.
And by your grace I live abundantly.
Your grace has made me totally free.

Because of your grace Lord I can forgive.
It's your grace that empowers me to live.
All because of your grace I am forgiven.
Your grace makes my prayer reach heaven.

Because of your grace Lord I have salvation.
Your grace has conveyed to me dominion.
And daily I receive your celestial protection.
Your grace affords me abundant provision.

By your grace Lord I receive divine favour.
Your grace affords me a good name and honour.
With your grace on my life I'll fulfil destiny.
And I will live with you in heaven eternally.

For me dear Lord your grace is sufficient,
It's more than enough and extremely efficient.
It's all that I need and more than I deserve,
To live successfully and to be preserved.

Memory verse: 2 Cor. 12:9
And he said unto me, My grace is sufficient for thee: for
my strength is made perfect in weakness. (KJV)

Light it up!

(Matthew 5:13-19)

God's light is like a candle,
That's blowing in the wind.
The storms of life it can handle,
For His light will never dim.

God's light is like a useful torch.
When suddenly power goes.
This small light penetrates the dark,
And everybody knows.

God's light is like a great big fire,
That got started with a small spark.
It spreads and spreads on forever,
Illuminating the dark.

God's light is like a light house,
A signal to ships off their course.
He's hoping that they will follow the light,
And return home if they're lost.

Memory verse: Matthew 5:16
Let your light so shine before men, that they may see your good works, and glorify your Father which is in heaven. (KJV)

Ask, Seek and Knock

(Matthew 7:7-12)

Ask and keep on asking,
Seek and you shall find,
Knock and keep on knocking,
The keys to the kingdom are mine.

Ask and keep on asking,
And please do say thank you,
Do not be anxious for anything,
God will take care of you.

Seek and keep on seeking,
The Lord while He may be found,
For there will soon come a day,
When the chances are all gone.

Knock and keep on knocking.
On heavens open door,
Graciously He pardons,
Abundantly He'll pour.

Please do unto others,
As you wish them do to you,
Whatever actions you mete out,
Will be meted back to you.

Pray and keep on praying,
From the rising of the sun,
Praise and keep on praising,
Even when the sun goes down.

Memory verse: Math 7:7-8
Ask, and it shall be given you: seek, and ye shall find; knock, and it shall be opened unto you: For everyone that asketh receiveth; and he that seeketh findeth; and to him that knocketh it shall be opened. (KJV)

Charity

(1 Corinthians 13)

I can converse in many different languages;
French; je t'aime and Spanish if you wish.
Trinidad creole I can speak with ease,
And a spiritual tongue, if you please.

I have the gift of prophesy;
Before things happen, I can foresee.
I have insights into God's secret plan,
Highly spiritual things, I can understand.

I have faith to move a mountain,
I believe that, without even doubting.
To the poor I will give my everything,
I will sacrifice my life and I'm not boasting.

But here's the twist that you must not miss,
Even if I can do all of this...
If I don't have love, which comes from above,
I really have nothing that I can speak off!

Love is patient, love is kind,
Some may say love is blind.
Love is strong and keeps no record of wrong,
In the good times and bad, love sticks around.

Love is not jealous or envious at all,
Love does not rejoice when someone has a fall.
Love never gives up, it never loses faith.
On us God's love patiently awaits.

Memory verse: 1 Cor. 13: 13
Three things will last forever-faith, hope and love-
and the greatest of these is love. (NLT)

Run to win.

(Hebrews 12:1-4)

The race is not for the swiftest,
But for him who endures to the end.
The path is not only for the fastest,
For sometimes it winds and bends.

We have a crowd of witnesses,
Who ran this race by faith.
They put aside and stripped off,
Every heavy weight.

Especially the sins,
That so easily trip us up.
And the struggles from within,
That tell us to quit and stop.

So let us run with patience,
This race set by God.
And show some endurance,
To obtain our reward.

Let's keep our eyes on Jesus,
The champion who ran before.
Despite the shame, He thought of us,
And the cross He did endure.

This race is an open one,
Everyone can run,
It's not a 100 meter dash,
But it's a marathon.

Don't get caught idling,
Watch out for traps of sin.
Daw your strength from within,
AND RUN THIS RACE TO WIN.

Memory Verse: I Cor. 9:24
Don't you realize that in a race everyone runs, but only
one person gets the prize? So run to win. (NLT)

The Minister

(Isaiah 61)

The Spirit of the Sovereign Lord,
Is upon Me, a Minister of God.
Anointed, appointed to proclaim,
The gospel of grace, through Jesus name.

To preach the good news to the poor,
Tell the broken hearted to mourn no more.
To declare freedom to those who are bound,
Announcing to all God's favour has come.

He gives us beauty in place of ashes,
And bestows His blessings as He wishes.
A blessed assurance for those that fear,
Praise Him and thank Him and never despair.

I have a double portion of His anointing,
And enough faith to remove a mountain.
The Lord Almighty makes this decree,
That in this land I shall have prosperity.

Memory Verse: Isaiah 61:7
Instead of shame and dishonour, you will enjoy a
double share of honour. You will possess a double
portion of prosperity in your land. (NLT)

The Good Shepherd

(John 10:1-18)

God gives to us our Pastors,
Anointed from above.
To nourish and nurture His sheep,
And to demonstrate His love.

Intercede on behalf of your Pastor,
For he is always under attack.
He needs the help of an intercessor,
To guard and watch his back.

Our God is the good shepherd,
Who loves His sheep of course!
He leaves behind the ninety-nine,
To look for the one that's lost.

Memory verse: John 10:11
I am the good shepherd: the good shepherd
giveth his life for the sheep. (KJV)

A Blessing or a Curse

(Deuteronomy 11:22-28)

I will keep God's commands,
And will walk in all His ways,
My heart and soul will love the Lord,
Forever His name I'll praise.

I will stand up for what I believe,
And to the Lord I would cleave,
The Lord shall surely wipe out,
My enemies without a doubt.

Wherever my feet shall walk,
Whatever my tongue shall say,
I will indeed possess it all,
It's the Lord's proven way.

No weapon can withstand,
It falls at the Lord's right hand,
Jehovah Nissi will see us through,
He's fighting for me and for you.

The Word of the Lord does say,
Choose you this day,
The blessing or the curse,
Please stop and think first.

Choose whom will you serve,
Do say, if you've got the nerve,
Choose life, choose Christ the Blessing,
If you reject Him, you'll die in your sin.

Memory verse: Deut. 11: 26
Look, today I am giving you a choice between
a blessing and a curse. (NLT)

Blessing After Blessing

(Deuteronomy 28:1-14)

And it shall come to pass...
If you obey God,
And do all that He asks,
That you shall be blessed;
In the east and the west,
From the north to the south,
This comes from God's mouth.

Blessings shall not only follow you,
But they will overtake you too,
To be blessed in whatsoever you do,
Whatever you put your hands to.

Blessed as the first and not the last,
Blessed to be at the head of your class,
Blessed with a healthy body,
Blessed to live life abundantly,
Blessed to give to somebody.

Blessed when you come in and when you go out,
Blessings enough to make you sing and shout,
Blessed are your animals and blessed is your crop,
Blessing after blessing, it's never going to stop!

The Lord will establish you and set you apart,
And the world will know that you have His heart,
The Lord shall open unto you His good treasure,
But you must abide in Him forever.

Memory verse: Deut. 28: 2
You will experience all these blessings if you
obey the Lord your God. (NLT)

I am in God's Army

(Ephesians 6:10-17)

You shall hear of wars and rumours of wars,
As the second coming of Jesus draws...
Closer! So put on your protective armour,
Be prepared and on guard soldier,
For when God gives the order.

Stand up! Stand tall and stand strong,
Don't let the enemy knock you down.
Guard yourself against the devil,
And all his attempts to do evil.
Against flesh and blood we do not wrestle.

The word of the Lord,
Is your spiritual sword.
Piercing every heart,
Bringing conviction, conversion, restoration,
Reconciliation and revelation.

His righteousness is our breastplate.
Quench fiery darts with the shield of faith.
His Word is your belt you'll agree,
And it gives to us all authority,
Against every lie of the enemy.

It's our freedom we are fighting for.
Against the ruler of darkness,
And all spiritual wickedness.
Against principalities, we wage war,
And every high thing we bring to the floor.

Stand therefore!
Put on the helmet of salvation.
Share the gospel in every nation,
On every radio and TV station.
The kingdom of God must take dominion.

Memory verse: Eph. 6:11
*Put on the whole armour of God, that ye may be able
to stand against the wiles of the devil. (KJV)*

A Child's Heart

(Matthew 18:2-6)

A child's heart is a heart;
That loves unconditionally,
Gives to others unreservedly,
Interacts with all indiscriminately,
Shares a hug compassionately,
Forgives offenders daily.

A child's heart is a heart;
That lives so very passionately,
Trusts in God whole heartedly,
Shares a smile wonderfully,
Gives a grin mischievously,
Listens to parents obediently,
Learns from examples quickly.

A child's heart is a heart;
That takes on the world confidently,
Approaches new tasks willingly,
Responds to questions non-hesitantly,
Embraces technology competently,
Adapting to change readily.

A child's heart is a heart;
That can be broken easily,
It must be handled delicately,
Cared for and nurtured lovingly,
For this is our God given responsibility.

Memory verse: Gal 3:26
For we are all the children of God by faith in Jesus Christ. (KJV)

Printed in the United States
By Bookmasters